POWERFUL — PF

Discover the Path

- Improve balance and bc
- Increase swing distance and accuracy
- Gain stamina and energy
- Calm the overactive, "critical" mind
- Avoid golf-related injuries to joints and spine
- Enjoy the game more ... even from the rough!

Golf pros everywhere are using and recommending yoga to provide a complete, comprehensive workout, aid in mastering the mental game and foster more consistent play. On and off the course, golfers who practice yoga enjoy greater confidence, power, and focus.

- Learn special breathing techniques to calm the mind and relax the body, leading to tireless, effortless play and greater shot distance and control
- Strengthen your core, enhance muscle memory and increase flexibility–reducing the risk of golf-related injury and shortening recovery time

Join professional golfers like Gary Player, Stewart Cink, Brad Faxon, Aaron Baddley, Jonathan Kyle, J.L. Lewis, Ty Tryon, Andrew Magee, Gary McCord, Julie Inkster, Betsy King and Jill McGill – all of whom have gained the competitive edge with the practice of yoga.

Illustrated, easy-to-follow, yoga-based fitness exercises help you find—and stay in—your zone. Lower your score and your blood pressure ... the easy way. *Play Better Golf with Easy Yoga*. Start today!

Play Better Golf with Easy Yoga

Yoga Fitness for Maximum Performance

© 2013 Patricia Bacall

Benesserra Publishing
1827 Barry Ave.
Los Angeles, CA 90025, 800-931-7007

First Edition
Paperback ISBN: 978-09884917-3-1
Ebook ISBN: 978-09884917-4-8

Publisher's Cataloging-In-Publication available on request

Disclaimer

Nothing contained in this book is intended to constitute, nor should it be considered as, medical advice or to serve as a substitute for the advise of a physician or other qualified health care provider. We make no assurances of the information being suited to your medical needs, and disclaim any implications that the content of this book is suitable for every person. Although the author and publisher have made every effort to ensure that the information in this book was correct at press time, they do not assume and hereby disclaim any liability to any party for any injury, loss, damage or disruption caused by errors or omissions, whether such errors or omissions result from negligence, accident or any other cause.

This book is not intended as a substitute for the advice and guidance of a qualified yoga teacher or the medical advice of physicians. The reader should regularly consult a physician in matters relating to his/her health, particularly with respect to any symptoms that may require diagnosis or medical attention. Learning yoga should be done with a qualified, experienced teacher; most importantly, common sense and caution should be used in embarking on any physically demanding endeavor.

Play BETTER GOLF
with Easy YOGA

GAIN POWER, FOCUS, ACCURACY, BALANCE and DISTANCE

Yoga Fitness for Maximum Performance

PATRICIA BACALL

Benesserra Publishing

Los Angeles, California

Introduction

As a steadfast, dyed-in-the-wool golf enthusiast, you already know you can enhance your game by spending lots of time on the putting green and driving range … and you probably already have. But you can improve your game even further by gaining an understanding of yoga and putting in a bit of time on the yoga mat.

This book shows you how yoga improves your golf game – and your entire life. It gives you an overview of yoga-based mental and physical conditioning that delivers the tools to generate more power, distance, speed, consistency, balance and concentration for maximum performance on and off the links.

I will help you integrate this simple, yoga-based fitness program into your golf training.

- You'll learn several poses that will enhance your strength, flexibility and range of motion for muscles you rely on for every putt or swing.
- You'll get more power, distance and satisfaction from your game through improved breathing, flexibility, strength, core conditioning, stability, and posture.

- And you'll discover that by tossing your specific golf goals off the fairway and learning to be present in the process, you can play a better golf game and enjoy your time on the links more.

Yoga hasn't been around for thousands of years by accident. People who practice yoga have long enjoyed an enhanced sense of awareness, improved physical fitness, and the alleviation of stress – all of which can add to your game.

And you don't need to turn yourself into a pretzel. Here you'll find easy yoga poses that almost anyone can achieve with no prior training. One of the beauties of practicing yoga is that you can adapt the poses to work with your specific fitness level. Poses become more advanced as you do, and you may be amazed at how quickly advancement can come with a regular yoga practice.

In addition to improving your physical game, you'll see how yoga is up to the important task of enhancing your mental game.

- You'll discover how easy it can be to stay calm, maintain a keen focus, utilize your breathing, and, most important of all, enjoy the sport even more than you do already.

- You might even be able to reduce the negative "chatter" that crowds your mind after making a nasty slice or missing an easy putt.

Probably no other game integrates as much mental and physical commitment as golf. A successful game demands that the mental hazards and constant struggle with the conscious mind – alert, logical and analytical, not to mention critical – be balanced with the subconscious mind, where intuition and muscle memory reside. However, golf gives you the perfect opportunity to become not only a better athlete, but also to become a more totally conscious person, transcending the mental turbulence created by the conscious mind, and achieving the "zone" mind state of pro golfers, accessible mainly through the subconscious.

It's sad, but true – golfers who fail to grasp the mental and emotional nuances of the game are doomed to languish in mediocrity, or get frustrated and give up the sport. *Play Better Golf with Easy Yoga* lets you master the mental and physical disciplines that golf demands by incorporating elements of an easy yoga practice.

Contents

9 Reasons to Practice Yoga for Golfers

Why Yoga for Golf? Here are the top 9 ways that yoga can improve your game:

1. Muscles Used in the Swing – How and why yoga affects them.

2. Fortifying Your Core – What it is, why you want it fortified and how yoga can do it.

3. Yoga, Your Stroke and Symmetry – Yoga is all about symmetry and so is your stroke!

4. Balance – Yoga is all about balance, another important aspect of golf.

5. Flexibility and Range of Motion – Improve both through yoga to improve your game.

6. Don't Forget to Breathe! – Yoga teaches you how to breathe as your body was meant to, an instant way to improve and sustain your energy.

7. Focus and Connect – How yoga can help your game when you stay in the moment and connect with the world around you (and that itty-bitty ball!).

8. All About Attitude – A crappy attitude generally results in a crappy game. Let yoga help you retain a positive attitude … even in a sand trap.
9. Overcoming Obstacles – Let yoga help you transform the "sand trap blues" into a welcome challenge.

Chapter 1

Why Yoga for Golf?

Top nine ways yoga can improve your game

Golf and yoga may seem like two entirely different activities, although the latter is actually linked to the former based on what it can do for your game. Below you will find nine ways yoga can improve your game, each of which is explored in greater detail throughout the book.

If you're ready for improvement, you're ready to go.

1. Your long drives will actually be long.

Ever hit the ball in what you thought was a long drive, look off into the distance to track it, only to find the ball is about 50 feet short of the tee? Well, misaligned club face may have something to do with it, but so does strength. A dynamic swing requires a big burst of strength, and yoga can help you achieve it.

Although yoga doesn't employ weights, resistance bands or any equipment typically used in strength training, you will get stronger with a regular yoga practice. That improved strength also lets you easily heft your golf clubs when you are without both caddy and golf cart for the day.

2. You'll lessen the risk of throwing out your back.

Even if you don't have a history of game-triggered injuries, you could be putting yourself at risk every time you take a swing if your core muscles aren't up to par. These important muscles in the central portion of your body help you move properly on every plane. You have three planes of motion with golf, and you have an easy and effective way to fortify your core with yoga. To become a healthy, injury-free golfer, your goal is a strong, stable body that is flexible and fluid. For some, flexibility or fluidity might be even more difficult to achieve than strength and stability. Stress and habitual ways of holding (armoring) your body contribute to a limited range of motion. The intrinsic, one-sided repetitive nature of the drive will likely cause your body structure to be unbalanced.

3. Your swing will no longer be off-center.

You may think your golf swing is all about the forward motion when you blast the club into the ball. It's not. Symmetry plays a huge part, with the most natural and effective swings being those that have a back swing that matches the swing through. A stance that is off-kilter by even a half an inch can be behind that persistent and irritating hook or slice. Yoga is huge on symmetry, and practicing it will help correct your over- or under-plane swing, just by the feel of it alone. As you gain greater kinesthetic sensitivity to your body through yoga awareness, you will be able to groove the optimal swing into your muscle memory.

Most of the poses are repeated so each side of the body gets equal time. Don't fret; you're not going to have to do everything in duplicate just to get symmetrical. But you will improve your symmetry, which in turn will improve your swing – and maybe even your ability to make an accurate center shot down the middle of the fairway.

4. You'll be able to make those one-footed shots from the rough.

Oh, that thing called balance! Like the core muscles, balance plays a major part in everything we do, and this counts triple when it comes to golf. It also affects you at a level deeper than not having a firm and balanced footing on the course.

Many golfers are not aware that their balance is poor, because they're accustomed to making subtle adjustments in their setup and throughout their swing to compensate for lack of balance. One way to determine if you're in balance is to hold your position at the top of the backswing or in the finish position of the swing. Can you stay there for 10 seconds? If you are not in balance, you'll start to topple like a bowling pin.

A good golf game requires your spine, as well as your swing, to be in balance, which helps your entire body stay balanced, giving you a consistent center of gravity. Balance can be flighty, too, always tempted to be thrown off by the slightest movement. Yoga teaches you how to fine-tune your balance so you are consistently stable, solid and grounded.

5. You'll be able to do your signature back flips after a hole-in-one.

Okay, your flexibility may not increase as much as that, but it will improve immensely. Flexibility is where you get the rotation and power to hit that long drive, and yoga is where you can get your flexibility. On your next practice shot, note how your shoulders rotate in relation to your hips. Your shoulders rotate 180 degrees from backswing to swingthough, and your hips turn 45 degrees. If you don't have that flexibility, you'd better hit the yoga mat.

6. You can do 18 holes – and be up for 18 more!

You know that sluggish feeling you get after a round of golf? It may soon be a thing of the past thanks, once again, to yoga. Yoga views the breath as your vital energy and teaches you how to use it to increase your vitality and sustain you for the long haul. Not only will your improved breathing increase your energy levels, it will help hone your concentration and calm your mind, skills that will translate off the course as well.

Freeing the flow of energy is contingent upon the golfer's ability to relax. When you can utilize your breathing to enter into a deep state of relaxation, you are able to experience being in the now, and your mind becomes clear. It is this freeing of stress that allows you to conserve your energy.

7. **Your putts will go near the green instead of somewhere near Greenland.**

You already know how important focus and concentration are in golf, and if you falter with either, your game is not all that great. Putts end up in strange places, drives end up in even stranger places, and you can even experience the golfer's nightmare of swinging and missing the ball entirely. Relaxed precision will change that. "Focus" is the last word you might think of when you consider the cliché images of the frustrated golfer breaking their clubs, swearing and squealing like a 5-year-old.

Ironically, when you take your focus off the outcome, with its self-imposed pressure to meet imaginary goals, your game will be more relaxed, precise and better.

With better precision and focus, you don't have to get really good at distracting people's attention so you can kick the ball you just missed onto the green. Instead, improve your focus and concentration with a solid yoga practice.

8. You'll stop throwing your clubs.

Anger, stress and headaches no longer have to be par for the course, so to speak. Even if your score is way above par, yoga brings down stress levels, enhances your mood and can transform an overall bad attitude into one of serene acceptance.

Hippie-speak mumbo-jumbo, you say? We say, regular yoga practice has been shown to affect certain brain chemicals and body proteins. It can increase the brain chemical GABA, for instance, and decrease the protein cytokine. Higher levels of GABA produce feelings of calm and reduced tension while low GABAs have been linked to depression. High levels of cytokine have been linked to moodiness and irritability.

One of my favorite anecdotes relates how Zen monks will practice archery for hours on end, attempting to master the physical aspects of the game. But it is not to win or achieve a particular score. When they have achieved mastery, they no longer practice, as they use it simply as the means to an end, a tool for reaching a particular level of consciousness. They are not attached to the outcome, not attached to winning or achieving a high or low score, and are thus free to enjoy more aspects of the entire experience.

9. You'll view sand traps and water hazards with a new appreciation.

Yes, you read that right. The golf course is full of obstacles just like life is full of obstacles. Yoga helps you overcome them and even view them with a new appreciation. Rather than looking at an obstacle as something to be avoided at all costs, if you do happen to get caught in one, you'll learn to view it as a challenge. Of course you'll still want to avoid the obstacles, but they will transform from being a thing to dread into something to embrace for their role as a guide in your life. Instead of a stumbling block, you'll see the water hazards as stepping stones to an increased appreciation of your problem-solving abilities and how you have learned to stay calm under pressure.

Before you start bending your clubs, you'll be able to call on yoga to connect with your breath and chronicle the various body sensations that occur in each moment. By observing your breath, you'll start to connect to feelings of being in the moment, nonjudgment and nonattachment. You'll clear the conscious mind and see and act with clarity. Yes, you read that right, too!

Chapter 2: Muscles Used in the Swing

How and Why Yoga Affects Them

If you think your golf swing uses only a few muscles on your arms, shoulders and back, think again. Your swing actually uses most of your muscles, some of which you may not even realize you have! Regardless of how small or seemingly unknown any of these muscles may be, yoga is going to affect them (in a good way, of course).

What Yoga Does for Your Muscles

While yoga enhances your overall physical fitness level, its effect on your muscles targets particular improvement in three areas: strength, flexibility and range of motion. Unlike other activities that may require three different movements to achieve three different benefits, yoga does it all for you in one fell swoop.

Muscle strength improvement becomes apparent when you get into and hold a yoga pose. Contracting certain muscles during a pose makes the opposing muscles relax, creating an instant resistance-free stretch. Such stretching is the secret behind the increase in flexibility, while your range of motion improves by consistently, yet gently, extending your muscles to their limits during each particular pose.

As you may have guessed, improving the strength, flexibility and range of motion involved in your golf swing can pay off tremendously on the course. To garner such an improvement, it's important to check out the specific muscles used in your swing, so you know what poses will help you most. A golf swing starts with your feet and ends with your hands, using dozens of muscles in between. According to speed training expert Dr. Larry Van Such, the forward swing alone uses approximately 22 muscles.

Upper body

Muscles of your arms and shoulders, plus the small muscles in your wrist known as the wrist flexors and extensors, play a major part in your swing. While the arms are used less to power the ball than the rest of the body, they help coordinate the initial and final stages of a swing, using the biceps, triceps and shoulder muscles to stabilize the club and keep it in line with the correct swing path.

To identify the individual muscles, move up your arm to find your elbow extensors and flexors that play a part in your swing, with the more common name of the former being the well-known triceps.

Move up your arm further still and you come to your deltoids, the shoulder muscles you knew would be part of your swing. Your swing also needs the chest muscles, or pectoralis major, and your back muscles, the latissimus dorsi. The pectoral and latissimus dorsi help stabilize the trunk during the backswing and forward drive.

Middle body

The body's midsection is where your core muscles reside, and they play a part in just about every movement you make, including your golf swing. The core and trunk muscles are key contributors in the takeback and forward swing. The oblique muscles aid in your body's backward coiling and forward uncoiling.

We explore the core in greater detail later in the book, but you should know the core consists of your abdominal, back and hip muscles, and those making up your rear.

Lower body

Your legs do more than just keep you off the ground; they have to power the rotation that happens in the hips, thighs and calves. Specific muscles involved include the front thigh muscles, or quadriceps, and the trio of inner thigh muscles known as the adductor brevis, adductor longus and adductor magnus. The "hammies" – your hamstrings – are major stabilization muscles even though they are not specifically used in the swing. The muscles involved in your lower leg are the tibialis anterior, gastrocnemius and soleus, which contribute to the upward drive during the forward swing.

Yoga Poses That Improve the 'Swing Muscles'

Yoga Pose 1: Downward Facing Dog

Downward Facing Dog (named because it resembles a dog stretching itself with its hind end up in the air and its front paws on the floor) is one of the most popular poses because it is also one of the most useful. It works your shoulders, arms, wrists, and legs. In addition to strengthening the muscles in the upper back, shoulders, and triceps, the pose reverses gravitational force on your upper body, strengthening your heart and creating more blood flow to your brain.

Downward Facing Dog will lengthen your spine, hamstrings, calves and the all-important Achilles tendons. When you bend over to tee up, you'll begin to notice the difference after only a few days.

How to do it:

1. Begin on your hands and knees (shoes off, of course). Align your wrists directly under your shoulders and your knees directly under your hips.

The fold of your wrists should be parallel with the top edge of your mat. Point your middle fingers straight forward.

2. Straighten your arms and relax your upper back.

3. Spread your fingers wide and press firmly through your palms and knuckles. Distribute your weight evenly across your hands. Avoid putting weight only on the outside of your hands.

4. Exhale as you turn your toes under so they have contact with the ground and lift your knees off the floor. Reach your tailbone up toward the ceiling, then draw your pelvis backward. Gently begin to straighten your legs, but do not lock your knees. Bring your body into the shape of an "A." Imagine your hips and thighs being pulled backwards from the top of your thighs. Do not walk your feet closer to your hands — keep the extension of your whole body. Keep at least 3 or 4 feet of distance between your hands and feet.

5. Press the floor away from you as you push your pelvis back. As you lengthen your spine, lift your sit bones up toward the ceiling. Now press down equally through your heels and the palms of your hands.

6. Rotate your arms externally opening up your elbow creases to face front. Wrap your triceps tightly outward and toward your back.

7. Drop your chest toward your thighs as you continue to press the mat away from you, length-

ening and decompressing your spine.

8. Sink your heels toward the floor.

9. Relax your head, but do not let it dangle. Allow your gaze to go toward your feet.

10. Hold for 5-10 breaths. Always breathe in and out ONLY through the nose. Mouth breathing is discouraged in yoga in almost every tradition.

11. To release, exhale as you gently bend your knees and come back to your hands and knees.

You should feel this pose throughout your shoulders and legs. If not, pull your shoulder blades more actively toward your spine while in the pose and press your thighs and legs backward more strongly, but do not lock your knees. Root firmly through your feet on the mat.

Your calves will probably feel this as much or more than any other part, and this is good. With Downward Facing Dog, you'll wake up those calf muscles, and stretch out your Achilles tendons.

As a bonus from this most basic pose, you'll get a flood of fresh, oxygenated blood to your brain, so don't be surprised if you want to start howling at the next tee.

Yoga Pose 1A: Half Downward Facing Dog

This modification will help rehabilitate rotator cuff and wrist injuries.

To strengthen your rotator cuff muscles with Half Downward Facing Dog, place the heels of your palms flat on the wall at about waist height, and walk your feet back directly under your hips as you bend forward with your head between your arms and your spine parallel to the floor. Keeping both hands firmly pressed into the wall, wrap your triceps to the outside so the heads of your upper arm bones engage in your shoulder sockets. (Firming up the triceps is another way to think of this last tweak.) Stay here for approximately 30 seconds to one minute, breathing deeply.

Click here for link to video of Half Downward Facing Dog

Half Downward Facing Dog with golf club

Yoga Pose 2: Plank

This pose is key to increasing strength and stability in your core. In addition to increasing strength in your shoulders, legs, stomach, and back, Plank pose gives your arm and wrist muscles a major workout.

How to do it:

The pose looks like the top of a basic military style pushup, except you not go up and down. Instead, keep your body straight as a plank at the top of the pushup.

1. Start on your hands and knees as with Downward Dog, with your palms directly beneath your shoulders.

2. Extend your legs, keeping your toes tucked under. Straighten your arms, keeping your back straight and your body positioned – you guessed it – like a plank above the mat.

3. Rather than looking down toward your navel or forward, keep your gaze focused slightly ahead of your hands, so that your neck stays in a straight line with your spine.

4. Hold for at least 30 seconds while breathing deeply through your nose.

Modification: This variation on Dolphin Plank pose is useful if your wrists are being overworked in straight-arm Plank pose:

• Lower your forearms to the floor and keep your hands clasped or your palms flat.

• Keep your body in a straight plank as much as possible from your heels to your shoulders, and avoid allowing your belly to sag down toward the mat.

• Keep pulling in your abdominal muscles while at the same time lowering your hips, and you'll see how challenging it can be to simply hold up your own body weight.

Dolphin Plank pose takes stress off wrists. (see p.44)

Yoga Pose 3: Chair

Chair Pose is a powerful standing yoga posture that strengthens the back, thighs and lower body. The pose appears as if you are sitting in a chair with your arms raised. Your thighs seem to be doing most of the work, but Chair pose actually works approximately 70% of your body, because your upper and lower back are engaged as well as your legs, abs, shoulders and arms.

An added bonus is the cardiovascular stimulation it gives to your heart and lungs. Therefore, the Chair is excellent for raising your heart rate and increasing your metabolism.

How to do it:

1. Stand with your feet shoulder-width apart and your spine straight. As you inhale, raise your arms to an approximate 45-degree angle to the ground. Face your palms toward each other with your fingers extended. Move your shoulders down and back, and engage your abdominal muscles.

2. Take a breath. Exhale and begin to sit, bending your knees and bringing your thighs as close to parallel to the ground as you can. Your torso will angle a bit over your thighs, which is fine, as is having your knees project a bit over your feet. Try to make a right angle between your calves and thighs, and then another right angle between your thighs and your body. Keep your inner thighs parallel to each other.

3. Hold the pose for at least 30 seconds, breathing in and out through your nose, and work on lengthening the time you hold the pose to 1 minute. Keep your breathing deep as you work the largest muscles in your body (if you need to breathe faster, that's okay.) Release the pose by inhaling and straightening your knees.

If you're feeling the tension in your thighs, you're doing it right. If you're not feeling much in your upper body, try stretching your arms up a little higher. Make sure you do not hunch up your shoulders; instead, slide your shoulder blades down your back.

Yoga Pose 4: Restorative (Resting) Pose – Child's

Child's Pose is a relaxing pose you can use to rest between the more challenging postures; however, it's also important in its own right for its ability to stretch the hips and spine, expand the lungs, relax tension in the neck, lower blood pressure and relieve gas.

How to do it:

1. Kneel on the floor, with the tops of your feet on the floor. Touch your big toes together and sit on your heels, then separate your knees about as wide as your hips.

2. Exhale and lower your torso down between your thighs. Rest your forehead on the mat. Breathe deeply into your lower back to broaden your sacrum across the back of your pelvis. Lengthen your tailbone down and away from the spine while you tuck your chin down slightly to lengthen your neck. Even though your lungs are in a difficult position to breathe into the front of your body, you will begin to notice all kind of space between your ribs and back into which you can breathe, increasing your capacity into that little-used area of your lungs.

3. Lay your arms on the floor alongside your torso, hands pointing behind you, palms up, and release

the fronts of your shoulders toward the floor. Feel how the weight of the front shoulders pulls the shoulder blades wider across your back.

4. Stay here anywhere from 30 seconds to a few minutes. To come up, lengthen the front torso, press the hands into the floor under your shoulders, and slowly sit up, allowing time for your blood pressure to normalize.

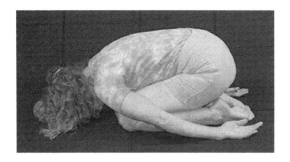

Arms can be back by hips or in front of shoulders.

Chapter 3: Fortifying Your Core

What It Is, Why You Want It Strong, and How Yoga Can Do It

You sit. You bend. You breathe. And you can only do all these basic things because of those things called your core muscles. Lots of hype has been swirling around the core, with training circuits and stability exercises and murmurs of "core this and core that" on the tips of many trainers' tongues. While this is one instance where the hype is warranted, you don't need massive amounts of circuits and training to strengthen your core. You can fortify it with yoga and help your golf game at the same time.

Your Core Explained

Your core muscles are those deep within the center of your body that form a cylinder, kind of like a natural girdle of armor. They make up your inner foundation, supported by the main muscle groups transversus abdominis, multifidus, perineum (pelvic floor muscles), internal and external obliques, serratus anterior, rectus abdominis, erector spinae and the diaphragm. While not specifically core muscles, the hip adductors are very important, including the adductor longus on the inside of the thigh, and gluteus medius and maximus.

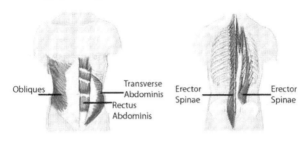

Obliques | Transverse Abdominis | Rectus Abdominis | Erector Spinae | Erector Spinae

Illustration courtesy of http://www.splitsecondbasketball.com/movement/4-reasons-your-basketball-training-must-include-core-work/

Even if you are not familiar with this spate of official names, rest assured you're familiar with the muscles themselves. You also use them daily unless, of course, you make it a regular habit never to walk, stand, sit, bend or breathe.

Transversus Abdominis

These guys exist in the deepest recesses of your abdomen, right about in the area you pull when you're trying to gauge if you can pinch that proverbial inch. Their job is to form a kind of belt around your middle, connecting the lower vertebrae to each other and then wrapping around your sides, ending up in the middle front of your abdomen.

To get in touch with these muscles, exhale deeply and hold the exhalation. Feel how your spine is instantly stabilized and your abdomen is just as instantly tight? That muscular girdle is your transversus abdominis at work.

Lumbar Multifidus

The lumbar multifidus are deep muscles that live on either side of your backbone. They connect the individual vertebrae to each other, stabilize your posture and let you bend and flex. These muscles are engaged when you set up for a shot, while you're bending forward. To feel them, inhale deeply and bend back from the waist, arching your back and tilting back your shoulders. That backward arch is also the multifidus in action.

Diaphragm

You probably remember the diaphragm from health class, or are at least are familiar with the name. It's responsible for your ability to breathe. This dome-shaped muscle sits beneath your lungs, forming the top of cylinder that is your core. When you're not giving the diaphragm the workout it deserves, your breathing is shallow.

Take a big, fat, deep inhalation. Hold it for a few seconds, then do an equally deep, fat exhalation. Continue to exhale, even when you think you have no breath left. Feel that deep push beneath your lungs that continues to press out the air? You are finally letting your diaphragm do its job! And when you deep breathe like this (but not pushing out the air) over and over again, voila! Your autonomous nervous system starts to slow down, your muscles relax and elongate, your brain starts to focus, and you, my friend, are at the gateway to the "zone"!

Pelvic Floor

For many people, the pelvic floor is a kind of dead area; they don't even know they have it. As the name suggests, the pelvic floor creates a base for the entire pelvic area, a hammock strong enough to hold babies in place while they're developing in the womb. These muscles are mainly responsible for supporting pelvic organs such as your bladder, rectum, prostate and, for women, reproductive organs. The same muscles also play some role in the working of the anal and urinary sphincters.

Men have a pelvic floor, too, although theirs may not be as celebrated. But believe me, neither sex wants to lose the elasticity of these muscles, which could contribute to urinary incontinence or prostate problems. Sometimes the muscles on the pelvic floor are too lax, making your swing flabby; sometimes they are too tight, which constrains hip flexibility.

The pelvic floor forms a sling that runs from the back of your body to the front, attaching at your tail bone in the back and slinging to the front of your pelvis. As the word "floor" implies, this muscle (perineum) makes up the bottom of the core cylinder when you contract it in conjunction with our pal transversus abdominis. It moves along with the diaphragm, and as you expand the abdomen with each breath, you should feel the pelvic floor lowering on your inhale and lifting on the exhale.

Exhale deeply and focus on contracting your pelvic

floor, feeling your transversus abdominis sink in to meet it. Inhale and let your muscles relax. You know that thing you do with your lower muscles when you have to go to the bathroom, but no facilities are around? That's your pelvic floor at work, and what a workout it can often get! Once you are able to connect with and strengthen the area, it provides enormous potential for both greater vitality and deep relaxation.

Obliques: They're Really Quite Straightforward

The internal and external obliques are two sets of muscles that run in opposite diagonal directions and overlap around the sides of the body. The primary function of the oblique muscles is to stabilize your core by aligning the ribs over the pelvis and holding this relationship in place. To effectively and efficiently create that twist in the torso, the hips have to engage the oblique abdominal muscles and use them to drive the upper body through the swing.

Gird Your Loins: Why You Want Core Fortification for Golf

For starters, keeping your core strong and stable will help keep you off the injured list. Minor tweaks and changes to the way you stand, the range of motion around the pelvis and the ability to twist your torso can add score-improving length to your drives and, of course, bragging rights.

Your swing relies heavily on your core muscles, as they help your body move properly on every plane. You've already seen how the multifidis help you arch your back; they're also responsible for your forward bends. The other two planes you use during your swing are the side-to-side motion and the twist, or rotation. A strong, stable core translates to a strong, stable swing. It helps you maintain proper posture during any activity, golf-related or not.

Yoga Poses for Core Strength

Yoga Pose 5: Side Bends

This side-bending pose stretches and strengthens the sides of the body, spine, shoulders, armpits and belly. It tones the thighs, improves digestion and helps relieve tension, anxiety and fatigue. It also creates more space in the chest for your breath, which expands your lung capacity, adding to your stamina and energy. As a bonus, it even trims your waist.

How to do it:

1. Begin by standing with your feet together and your arms at your sides. If you have trouble balancing, stand with your feet 6 inches apart or wider.

2. On an inhalation, sweep your arms out to the side and then up overhead. Turn your arms so your palms face each other. Straighten your arms completely, but do not lock your elbows. Interlace your fingers and point your index fingers toward the ceiling.

3. Exhale as you press your left hip to the side. Slowly start to bend your arms and upper torso to the right. Keep your feet grounded and your thighs firm and engaged. Lift up and out through your entire spine and arms. Keep your chin up and away from your chest, looking straight ahead. Try to keep your body on a flat plane as you bend sideways; avoid turning your left shoulder toward the ground or twisting your body.

4. Hold for five breaths, inhale, and come back to center. Then bend to the left, and come back to center. Exhaling, sweep your arms back down to the sides of the body.

Side bend with club

1. Hold on to the club with thumbs touching.

2. Follow the instructions for basic Side Bend.

3. Hold for 20-30 seconds, breathing.

Yoga Pose 6: Bridge

Bridge Pose is a gentle inversion that works with gravity to open the chest and shoulder area, strengthens the hips and lower back, engages the large muscles at the back of the thigh, and elevates the heart rate if held for 30 seconds or more.

How to do it:

1. Lie on your back with your knees bent and your

heels fairly close to your hips. If you were to reach your fingers down toward your heels, you'd just barely be able to graze your heels with your fingertips. You will notice, if you have difficulty lifting your hips, that you get the best leverage if your heels are directly under your knees.

2. Press your hips up toward the sky, attempting to make a straight "plank" from your knees to your shoulders, using your hamstring muscles and not your buttocks. Try to relax your butt and avoid squeezing.

3. If you can rock yourself from side to side and lift your body up enough to bring your upper arms behind your back and clasp your hands, this completes the pose and is a powerful opener for the chest muscles. If you can't do that, for now allow your arms to stay at your sides, and you will still gain significant benefit.

In addition to massaging the thyroid gland at the base of the throat, this pose engages the perineum muscle, which in turn stimulates both the testes and the ovaries. If you remember from the section on how important a strong core is, the perineum muscle is the muscle at the base of the body between the anal sphincter and the urogenital muscles. When you practice contracting this muscle, you are strengthening your pelvic floor muscles, which serves you in a variety of ways, including avoiding incontinence and improving sex.

Yoga Pose 7: Boat

This pose is exceptional for core fortification, and you'll be able to feel it working instantly. The Boat has you balancing on the area between your tailbone and sit bones with both your arms and legs raised in the air, as if your glutes (butt muscles) are the fulcrum of a seesaw.

How to do it:

1. Sit with your legs straight out in front of you and inhale deeply as you press your palms on the mat a bit behind your hips. Lift your chest toward the ceiling as you slightly lean back. Pull in your navel toward your spine.

2. Keeping your back straight, exhale and bend your knees, lifting your feet the floor. Inhale as you straighten your knees, if possible, keeping your legs at a 45-degree angle off the ground and your toes a bit higher than eye level.

3. Exhale deeply as you lift your arms forward, keeping them straight with fingers pointing toward your feet. Your arms should be parallel to each other. Inhale deeply as you pull your shoulder blades toward your spine and reach strongly through your fingertips.

4. Continue to breathe deeply and steadily as you hold the pose. Hold for at least 10 seconds at first, eventually working your way to a 1-minute stay. Always bring your legs back to the mat with a deep exhalation, followed with a deep inhalation as you sit upright back to the position in which you started.

Beginner's modification: Keep your knees bent and make your calves parallel to the floor.

Another modification option for sensitive backs: With knees bent and calves parallel to the floor, hold onto the sides of your thighs.

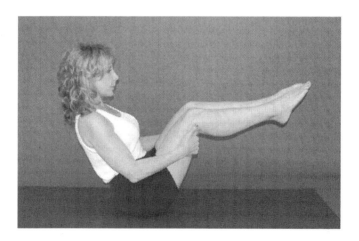

Yoga Pose 8: Crescent Lunge

Crescent Lunge pose strengthens your legs, stretching and opening your hips. It also gets your heart rate up, which helps your overall conditioning and stamina.

How to do it:

1. Start in Downward Facing Dog. Inhale. Exhale and step your right foot forward between your hands, aligning your knee over your heel. Lower your hips into lunge position and shift your weight onto the ball of your back foot, bringing your hands to your hips. Keep your left leg strong and firm.

2. Stay up on the ball of your back foot and lift your upper body so you're standing straight up, inhaling as you raise your torso to upright. Go slowly to maintain your balance. If you have difficulty, keep your arms at your side. Once you are able to maintain your balance here, sweep your arms wide to the sides and raise them overhead, palms facing.

3. Be careful not to overarch the lower back. Pull in your navel. Lengthen your tailbone toward the floor and reach back through your left heel. Slide your shoulder blades down your back and firm up your triceps.

4. Do not allow the front ribs to press forward. Draw them down and into the torso. Lift the arms from the lower back ribs, reaching through your little fingers. Hold for 30 seconds to 1 minute.

5. Exhale, lower the torso to the right thigh, lower your hands back onto the floor, and, with another exhale, step your right foot back and return to Downward Facing Dog. Hold this pose for a few breaths and repeat with the left foot forward for the same length of time. After doing the pose on both sides, you may rest in Child's Pose if you like.

Yoga Pose 9: Twisting Crescent Lunge

Twisting Crescent Lunge pose is a challenging variation on the previous pose, a strength and balance posture that works toward creating stability throughout the entire body, but especially the core. Twisting the torso applies pressure to your internal organs, toning them and increasing their ability to detoxify your body. After twisting, your torso and digestive organs are flushed with oxygen-rich blood, which helps remove toxins while improving digestion. This pose also stretches and tones the legs, hips, and butt, and opens the chest, shoulders, and arms. It improves balance and increases both energy and confidence.

How to do it: (Note: Until you get to Step 7, the pose is the same as Crescent Pose)

1. Begin in Downward Facing Dog. With an exhalation, step your right foot forward between your hands.

2. Bend your front knee to 90 degrees, aligning your knee directly over the heel of your front foot. Your feet should be hip width apart with both feet facing forward, and your front shin should be perpendicular to the floor.

3. Come onto the ball of your back foot. Make sure your front shin stays vertical. Bring that foot forward as needed to make sure that your knee does not stick out past your ankle, as this strains the knee.

4. Lift your back knee. Straighten your back leg completely if possible. Keep the ball of your back foot firmly on the ground.

5. With your back leg strong and active, gently draw your left hip forward as you press your right hip back, squaring your hips so they are parallel to the top edge of your mat.

Beginner's Modification: If it is too difficult to keep your back leg raised, lower your knee to the floor and slide your leg back a few inches. Un-tuck your back toes and rest the top of your back foot on the floor if your knee is down.

6. Inhale as you raise your torso to an upright position. Sweep your arms overhead. Draw your tailbone toward the floor. Rotate your pinky fingers toward each other, opening your arms so your palms face each other. Gently tilt your head and gaze up at a space between your thumbs.

Now continue into Twisting Crescent Lunge:

7. Lower your arms and bring your palms together in prayer position at your chest.

8. Exhaling, twist your torso to the right so that your left shoulder is pointing down toward your right knee. Bring your left elbow to the outside of your right thigh.

9. Press your upper left arm against your thigh and turn your chest to the right.

10. Tuck your tailbone under and engage the muscles of your abdomen to help stabilize your core.

11. Extend and stretch up through the crown of your head, lengthening your upper body. Draw your shoulder blades down and firm them into your upper back.

12. Hold for up to 1 minute, breathing deeply. Exhaling, release your hands back to the mat and step back into Downward Dog. Repeat on the other side.

Rest in Child's Pose if you like.

Yoga Poses 10 & 10A:
Dolphin and Dolphin Plank

Starting out in Dolphin Pose works the shoulders and triceps, and dropping down into Dolphin Plank Pose works your entire core. As you advance, it is possible to switch back and forth between Dolphin and Dolphin Plank Pose for a more extreme core-strengthening workout.

And this fantastic fitness tool uses the weight you always have available to you – your body!

Dolphin Pose

How to do it:

1. Come onto your mat on your hands and knees. Set your knees directly below your hips and your forearms on the floor with your shoulders directly above your wrists. Firmly press your palms together and your forearms into the floor. You can

also either clasp your hands together or place your palms face down.

2. Curl your toes under, then exhale and lift your knees away from the floor. At first keep the knees slightly bent and the heels lifted away from the floor. Lengthen your tailbone away from the back of your pelvis and keep your navel pulled in.

3. Continue to press the forearms actively into the floor. Firm your shoulder blades against your back, then widen them away from the spine and draw them toward the tailbone. Hold your head between the upper arms; don't let it hang or press heavily against the floor.

4. Straighten your knees if you can, but if your upper back rounds it's best to keep them bent. Make your back as flat as possible and continue to lengthen your tailbone away from your shoulders.

5. Stay in the pose between 30 seconds to one minute. Then release your knees to the floor with an exhale.

Yoga Pose 10A: Dolphin Plank Pose

How to do it:

1. Start in Dolphin Pose, knees bent. Walk your feet back until your shoulders are directly over the elbows and your torso is almost parallel to the floor.

2. Press your forearms and elbows firmly against the floor. Firm your shoulder blades against your back and spread them away from the spine. Similarly spread your collarbones away from the sternum.

3. Press the back of your thighs toward the ceiling and your tailbone toward the floor as you lengthen it toward the heels. As always, in a core strengthening pose, pull your navel in toward your spine.

4. Straighten out the back of the neck and look straight down at the floor, keeping the jaw and eyes soft.

5. Stay in the pose anywhere from 30 seconds to 1 minute, breathing in and out through the nose.

6. Release your knees to the floor with an exhale. To counteract core fatigue, rest in Child's Pose.

Chapter 4:
Yoga, Symmetry and Your Stroke

Yoga Is All About Symmetry, But How Important Is It to Your Game?

Golfers sometimes become obsessed with symmetry. You've heard the drill: "Stand square to the target, turn the shoulders 90 degrees, the hips 45 degrees, have the club parallel at the top, and the club face square at impact."

While these are all important points for creating the fundamentals of the golf swing, will they make the ball go farther and put it where you want? Yes … unless thinking of all these bits and pieces of advice during your swing cause it to become too tight and over-controlled.

When your stroke is symmetrical, your placement will be more accurate and distance more effortless, while your body endures less strain and stress. To this end, you want to first begin to notice asymmetry related to your swing, and then begin to counteract the tension that your body has learned to work around by using strengthening poses on the weaker side, and opening poses on the stronger, but possibly tighter side of your body.

Symmetry in golf exists in more places than on the perfectly dimpled golf ball. It also exists in a perfectly executed swing. The attention and care you pay to your backswing should not end once the club hits the ball. Your swing-through needs to be as precisely executed as your backswing, with movements that mirror the backswing and, you guessed it, create lovely symmetry. At least that's the way it should be if you want a swing that does more than make the ball go a few feet in a random direction.

Instead, giving your swing symmetry can result in a powerful and efficient blast that makes the ball fly a few hundred feet in the direction you actually intend.

Spot Checking Symmetry

To spot check if you're already giving your swing the symmetry it needs, go through the motions of your swing in your head, or even in the room if there's not a lot of breakables in your path and you happen to have a golf club lying around.

To really get a feel of the symmetry going on in your swing, go through the swing motions you already know quite well, but pay attention to how many times symmetry is created. This exercise in visualization will aid in symmetry since you'll be keenly aware of the multiple times it happens.

A typical right-handed swing starts with you grasping the club in front of you with both hands and extended arms. You move the club over your right shoulder as your right arm bends away from the club and your left arm is straight and at a 90-degree angle to the club. The club reaches its peak behind your shoulder and then comes down, hitting the ball, and continuing to move to create the swing-through after you hit the ball.

Like the backswing, the swing-through should bring the club over your shoulder with one arm bent away from the club and the other arm straight. This time the club is over your left shoulder, and your left arm bends away from while your right arm is straight until the club is behind you.

Review the motions again, counting the number of times symmetry comes up. The most obvious is the backswing mirroring the swing-through, giving us one big example of symmetry.

Then there's the symmetry of the arms mirroring each other when they are in front of you at the onset of the swing, taking the total to two, and the right and left arms mirroring each other when they are bent over your shoulder in the backswing and again in the swing-through—symmetry examples three and four.

A solid putt should also employ symmetry if you want to enjoy the outcome. Once again, your extended arms in front of you mirror each other, followed by the backswing that is mirrored by the swing-through, throwing more symmetry into the mix. If it all works together, you'll get the chance to see your ball go closer to the hole than you may have ever imagined possible.

Yoga and Symmetry

The repetitive nature of the golf swing tends to make your body lopsided over time. But now that you can clearly see how important symmetry is for your golf game, you'll love what yoga can do for you. Not only will it help you with symmetry on the physical level, but it can touch on symmetry in your mental and spiritual state.

Let's start with the physical. Yoga's symmetrical approach to balancing the body is apparent in almost every pose. A prime example is Kneeling Spinal Balance Pose.

Yoga Pose 11: Kneeling Spinal Balance

This pose points out how asymmetrical your body might be and helps to make it more symmetrical, as it develops your balance and right/left brain integration. Just be sure you aren't trying to do the impossible and balance on the same side leg and arm!

How to do it:

1. Begin this pose on your hands and knees, with your palms flat against the mat and your knees and shins also firmly on the mat, your knees directly under your hips.

2. Inhale and lift and extend your right arm straight out in front of you as you lift and extend your left leg straight out behind you. Keep breathing as you hold the pose there.

3. Look straight down at your left thumb on the mat – do not look at the lifted hand, because doing so might create problems in your neck. Reach out with the extended hand as far as you can, as if you were going to shake hands with someone. The foot in the back is flexed with the toes pointed downward and stretched out through the heel. Note how the symmetry (or asymmetry) of your extended arm and leg feels. Breathe.

4. Inhale deeply and release back to hands and knees on the exhale. Inhale and repeat the pose with the opposite arm and leg extended. Work up to holding this pose for 30 seconds on each side.

Notice if you feel a difference between the two sides as you do the pose the second time.

Yoga has its fair share of what are known as asymmetrical poses that focus on one half of the body, but such poses are meant to be done twice. One run-through focuses on the right side while the other focuses on the left side, leaving you once again dancing with your new friend, symmetry.

Moving Towards Awareness of More Symmetry

As alike as each half of your body might seem to be, keep in mind that absolutely perfect symmetry does not exist. One side of your body may be tighter or less flexible than the other, something you can work on correcting through your yoga practice. Almost everyone has a stronger and weaker side.

The key point here is awareness. The better you get at noticing what you are feeling in your body during your yoga practice, the better you will be at noticing odd quirky feelings during your swing that results in a hook, slice or unintentional draw or fade. Your organs are not positioned perfectly symmetrical either; something to note if one side of your body reacts differently than the other.

It's important to honor each side of the body for the job it has to do. This extends to embracing the well-known yin and yang – the moon and sun – both of which are part of our makeup. The dichotomy is also seen in our dominant self and our shadow self, with the former typically on display for the world to see and the latter as our deepest, inner rebel. Just as the word "yoga" (union) implies, when we play golf, we are seeking to pull together the different parts of ourselves toward wholeness, including breath and movement, strength and flexibility, effort and relaxation. To play your best game, embrace both sides to form a single and symmetrical whole. This, of course, is true for your life both on and off the links.

Symmetry in Your Spiritual Nature

On the mental and spiritual level, yoga thinks of the body in terms of layers, with the physical layer as only one of five. Each layer is depicted with symmetrical form, our energy flows in a symmetrical pattern, and even the water molecules in our bodies become arranged more symmetrically as our energy changes for the better and our mood improves. That means all these underlying forces are working ... provided you take time to relax, breathe deeply, practice the poses and use yoga to prompt the vital forces to thrive in – say it with me now – symmetry.

Yoga Pose to Highlight Symmetry

Yoga Pose 12: Bound Angle

Bound Angle Pose is a powerful hip opener that lets you practice feeling symmetrical in an easy relaxed posture with your feet together in front of you and your knees bent out to the sides. By allowing the earth to support you in this pose, you can relax and begin to feel what symmetry feels like, or doesn't, depending on the state of your body.

How to do it:

1. Start seated with your legs straight out in front of

you. Inhale. Exhale deeply, open and bend your knees while you move your heels toward your sit bones. Continue your exhale as you place the soles of your feet together and drop your knees toward the mat as far as they drop naturally, which might not be very far if you are extremely tight in your inner thighs and groin.

2. Inhale and lengthen your spine toward the ceiling as you grasp each hand around each corresponding ankle, pulling your heels as close to your pelvis as possible. Exhale deeply as you ensure your pelvis is in a neutral position, neither jutting forward nor rolled back.

3. Inhale as you slide your shoulder blades down your back, and lengthen the front of your torso to open the chest. Breathe.

4. Hold the pose up to 3 minutes, concentrating on maintaining symmetry in your body positioning and your breath, with the depth of the inhales matching the depth of the exhales. Note which side of your body seems to be tighter or looser.

5. Release the pose on an exhale, moving your knees away from the floor and straightening your legs into your original seated position.

Note: if your inner thighs are so tight that you curl up like a shrimp when you open your knees, modify the pose by placing your hands behind your hips and sitting up as straight as possible. Find a position that you can hold for a few minutes and simply breathe, allow your knees to drop down, and open up your groin. Hello, inner thighs!

Another Bound Angle modification is to keep the soles of your feet together and your knees open to the sides, then lie down on your back. While most males have no issue sitting with their knees open, lying down in this position can be quite different. Just breathe and let your groin muscles relax and allow the adductor muscles in your inner, upper thighs to lengthen.

Chapter 5: Posture and Balance

Yoga, Golf and Yes, Life,
Are All About Balance

At the foundation of every good golf swing is good balance. Maintain your balance and you can deliver the clubhead to the ball with speed and accuracy. Lose your balance and your swing loses its tempo or rhythm, and falls apart.

Ten-time PGA Tour driving accuracy champion Calvin Peete says the three keys to straight driving are "balance, balance and balance." There are four main points during which you should check to see that you are balanced:

- At address, where your weight is equally balanced from side to side and front to back;

- At the top of the backswing, where you should be balanced on the back foot approximately 75%;

- At impact, where your weight shifts to approximately 75% on the front foot; and

- At the completion of the follow-through, where you

should be able to balance with 90% of your weight on the front foot, with the body again upright.

If you rush your swing, you will be off balance, resulting in inconsistent contact and poor ball flight. But if your weight shifts smoothly throughout the swing, your rhythm remains smooth and leads to more consistent impact, delivering more leverage and power.

Balance is not only important so you don't fall sideways after a hearty swing; it's an integral part of golf on both the physical and mental levels. Yoga relies very heavily on balance, and you can rely on yoga to improve your balance and your game. Let's start with balance on the physical level.

Your Posture and Physical Balance

Pay attention to your balance starts by paying attention to your spine to ensure it's in the proper position.

- A happy, healthy and properly positioned spine will keep you balanced whether you stand, sit, bend or twist.

- An improperly balanced spine can lead to leaning, listing, falling and all kinds of pain due to unnecessary stress hitting areas of your body that are not designed to support it.

Spot check the position of your spine by standing up straight and tall. Your vertebrae should align straight up your back (although of course, it is not as flat as a board). You have three natural back curves: a slight forward curve at your neck, a slight backward curve in your upper back and a slight forward curve in your lower back.

"Proper" posture means standing or sitting with your back straight, your shoulders and hips even and square, your weight evenly distributed on each foot and your chest held high. Proper posture helps you maintain your back's natural curves; improper posture distorts it.

During naturally good alignment, your ears should be over your shoulders, and if you were to drop a plumb line from your ear lobe like an earring, it would fall just between your instep and heel.

A good exercise for aligning your spine involves imagining a string running through your backbone, out the top of your head and up toward the sky.

- Take a deep inhale and imagine the string establishing itself in your spine.
- Now deeply exhale and feel the string extend from your tailbone to the sky, straightening your back and aligning your posture. It feels like you just got a few inches taller, doesn't it?
- Now imagine the string breaks and your body collapses. Your spine becomes more like cooked spaghetti than that fine ramrod you previously emulated. Your chin juts out, your shoulders stoop forward, your chest becomes concave. Your stomach bulges, and your head dangles in front of

your spine instead of being perched on top of it — not a pretty sight.

Keep that misaligned posture intact as you walk around a bit. Now attempt a set up to address the ball using that exaggerated slouch. It would be nearly impossible to hit a good drive with your posture like that, right? It's comical! But that's how we go through a lot of our day.

Now sit down and imagine you're at your computer. If the stooped-forward posture feels familiar, you're out of alignment. And you are certainly not alone. Many folks toil at their desks day after day with their posture completely out of whack, and then must spend a lot of money and time at the physical therapist's or chiropractor's office when their backs suddenly "go out."

The mess can extend to other daily activities, such as leaning forward and slouching while driving, standing or walking around with your head hung low, sleeping in a curled-up position and propping your neck up on a pillow when you read in bed. Not only does the back of your neck get unnaturally stretched out, your pectoral muscles shrink and tighten, closing down your chest.

All these small actions done with poor posture can add up in a big way to contribute to a misaligned and unbalanced spine. You can be sure such flaws affects your balance, your swing, and your entire game. Yoga to the rescue once again!

Yoga Pose to Open the Chest

Yoga Pose 13: Cobra

A closed-down chest is one of the unsavory side effects of the ongoing postural stoop. Yoga helps correct that with a pose that opens the chest, which in turn, automatically opens the shoulders and stretches the spine.

Meet the Cobra, so called because the top half of the body is curling upward from the ground while the hips and legs remain in contact with the ground, resembling a serpent ready to strike. This pose looks simple, but the way to do it properly is not to overdo lifting the chest. Anyone can lie on their stomach and straighten their arms, but this will definitely put undue pressure on the lumbar vertebrae (lower back).

The key to doing the Cobra while protecting your lower back is to keep the hips down and concentrate on curling up through the thoracic vertebrae in your mid- to upper back.

How to do it:

1. Exhale deeply and lie on your stomach, stretching your legs back and keeping the tops of your feet on the mat.

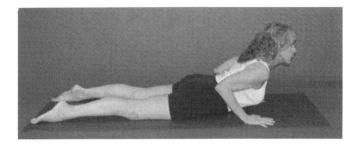

2. Inhale and place your palms on the mat next to your ribs, with the heels of your palm approximately level with your floating ribs, spreading your fingers, and hugging your elbows to your sides.

3. Exhale deeply as you press your pubis, tops of thighs, and feet firmly into the mat.

4. On an inhale, begin to lift your chest off the floor using your back muscles, as you keep your thighs and feet firm against the mat. Don't go overboard–Cobra pose is not a pushup.

5. Begin to straighten your arms, but do not lock the elbows. Keep your elbows pressing into the sides of your waist. Feel the slight backbend throughout the length of your spine. Look straight ahead, or if it feels natural to you, slightly upward. Breathe.

6. Slide your shoulder blades down and away from your ears, firmly against your back. Continue to inhale and exhale deeply as you hold the pose up to 30 seconds.

7. Exhale as you release back to the original position. Take Child's pose if you want to feel a counter-stretch to the arching of the back.

Notice the openness you feel in the front of your body while in Cobra pose. Recall the openness and freedom you are finding to help you achieve and maintain proper posture on the course and throughout your daily activities.

Physical Balance and Your Swing

As you may have guessed from all this, your spine and body alignment play a big role in balance during your swing. While you know you don't want to stand up ramrod straight while you take your swing, you do want to keep your spine at a set angle and maintain a solid center of gravity throughout each phase of the stroke.

You are already aware of all the elements that play a part in your swing, and as you may also have discovered, maintaining balance in each of these elements is key to maintaining balance as a whole.

The other factors that contribute to your balance are the position of your head, the flex in your knees, your grip and your stance width. Your body weight's distribution through your feet tops off the balance sheet. As you probably also already know, proper balance for your swing places your weight distribution through the balls of your feet and your heels – never on your toes.

When you are properly balanced with your weight over the arch of your foot, and push your hips back about 5 inches (or at least as far as you're tilting forward), you will be able to keep your back straight, and your club shaft at a right angle to your back. Your swing will feel effortless.

Mental Balance

As physically balanced as your body may be during your game, you can still ruin your shot if your mind isn't as balanced. Mental balance in golf involves an emotional and mental steadiness that keeps you focused, alert, and able to play at your fullest potential. Yoga helps with both the mental and physical balance, keeping you solid, stable, and grounded in both your body and mind. Here's where you have to apply your will, discipline yourself to stay positive, and not let your mind start running down a rut of negativity or self-deprecation. Even if you are in the rough, with a score-crunching lie that tripped you up the last time, now is *not* the time to relive that scenario in your mind. Bring your awareness back to your breath, focus your concentration on the ball, and simply allow your body to do what it knows how to do already.

Yoga Pose for Balance

You've already met one of the most famous yoga poses with Downward Facing Dog, and now you're meeting another one with the Tree Pose, which has you standing tall and strong like a tree while balancing on one leg. Ready?

Yoga Pose 14: Tree and Modified Tree

How to do it:

1. Inhale deeply and stand tall with your feet firmly on the mat, shoulder width apart. Touch your palms together in front of your heart. Find a spot on the wall or ground on which to focus, and softly gaze at that focal spot. Exhale and

gently shift your weight to your left foot, without pushing that hip out of alignment (keep lifting your body up, rather than sinking down into the hip). Firm that foot into the floor, while you bend your right knee and bring the arch of the right foot to the calf of the left leg. (Do not press your heel against the inside of the knee, place it just under the knee, so that your arch is touching your calf muscle.) Inhale and find your balance here.

2. Exhale deeply, checking that the center of your pelvis is directly above your left foot on the floor and that your pelvis is in a neutral position, neither tilted forward nor back. Keep the standing leg as straight as possible, or it will be difficult to balance.

3. Inhale deeply, lengthening your spine as you press your right foot firmly against your left calf and your left foot more firmly into the mat. Imagine that string again going up through your spine and lift

through the crown of your head toward the sky.

4. Gazing at your focal spot, breathe deeply, with even, measured inhalations and exhalations as you hold the pose for up to 1 minute. For a greater challenge, begin to allow your hands to rise and "branch out" until your arms are raised straight up or slightly out, aligning your elbows with your ears.

5. Exhale deeply, lower your hands to your heart, and return to standing with both feet on the mat; take a couple of breaths, and repeat on the other side.

A note on the focal point:

Focusing on a fixed point in the distance helps balance immensely, both for your physical and mental states. To further explore its importance, try Tree pose again, but instead of focusing on a fixed point as Step 4 suggests, look around in a random fashion or switch your gaze from one object to another. Fall over yet?

Beginners Modification: Until you can balance on one leg, keep the toe of the free leg (the one on which you are NOT standing) touching the ground.

Focusing on a fixed point helps keep you grounded and stable. It also keeps your mind protected from any chaos and distractions that may be going on around you. The concept works on both the literal and figurative levels and can give your golf game a real boost.

Chapter 6:
Flexibility and Range of Motion

Improve Both through Yoga and Improve Your Game

"Blessed are the flexible, for they shall not be bent out of shape." — Unknown

You already know power is a major factor in a swing that can send your golf ball soaring. But you may not know that full power can come only from full flexibility. Flexibility helps you extend your muscles, optimize your range of motion, and pack your swing with everything you've got.

Go through the motions of your swing to check it out. Gear up for your backswing but only rotate and extend back about half the distance you normally do. Now go for the swing-through, mirroring your back-swing and has now also been limited to about half the distance you normally employ.

Can you imagine how poor your shot would be with only half of your current flexibility and range of motion? Now imagine how much more powerful your shot will be when you increase your flexibility and range of motion by even a small amount. Yoga can certainly help you obtain the increased flexibility and range of motion you need to enhance the power of your swing.

Flexibility vs. Range of Motion

Before we continue, let's clear up the difference between flexibility and range of motion.

- Flexibility refers to your muscles' pliability, or their ability to repeatedly stretch, extend and contract without injury.

- Range of motion, often abbreviated as ROM, is the measurement of a joint's movement from its full flexion to its full extension.

- Flexion is just a fancy term for the joint in its bent state where the bones forming the joint are closest together, such as a bent elbow.

Flexibility is one key to ensuring your ROM is at its optimum range, although ROM is also affected by other factors. These include your age and gender, the joint structure, the state and type of connective tissue, muscle bulk, past injuries and even your internal environment. For instance, your sluggish body has a much lower ROM when you first wake up than after a hot bath or shower.

Flexibility and PNF

Another factor affecting your flexibility is a fancy concept called Proprioceptive Neuromuscular Facilitation, but you can call it PNF. To make it simple, imagine the ability to stretch your muscles a little bit farther than you thought you could. PNF goes into action if you contract a muscle when it's nearly at its maximum length, which eases the pressure on your muscle spindles and sends a signal to your body that it's okay to stretch a little deeper.

Think of PNF as a protective mechanism hard-wired into your brain that simply does not allow you to flail your limbs around willy-nilly, stretching out like Gumby. Without a supporting contraction, your stretch is limited because the signal sent from your body to your mind and back again is saying a deeper stretch is not safe.

PNF can be a boon for the additional flexibility that transforms your swing from good to astounding. You can try out the concept with yoga's Standing Forward Bend.

Yoga Pose 15: Standing Forward Bend

How to do it:

1. Stand with your feet shoulder-width apart and your hands on your hips. Inhale. Exhale deeply

and bend forward from the hips, not the waist. As your upper body descends, focus on lengthening the front of your torso. Keep your neck in line with your back, looking neither up nor down as you bend forward. And, no matter what any gym coach ever told you, DO NOT BOUNCE!

2. Depending on your flexibility, place your palms or fingertips on the mat, a yoga block or even the seat of a chair. If you cannot bend far enough to touch the floor, place your palms on your shins. You can also cross your forearms and hold your elbows if that feels right.

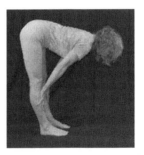

Figure 1, set up for forward bend
Figure 2, beginner forward bend

3. Deeply inhale and exhale as you hold the pose. Use each deep inhalation as a chance to slightly lift and elongate the muscles in your torso. Use each deep exhalation to extend and release a bit more fully into the forward bend. When you feel that you've dropped down just about as far as you can, begin to pull up on the muscles in the front of the thigh. Herein lies the

PNF at work. Notice how contracting the antagonistic muscles in the front of your thighs can actually give you a deeper stretch in the hamstrings.

Figure 3, intermediate forward bend
Figure 4, advanced forward bend

4. Now, firm up all the muscles in your legs, and begin to stand erect with a deep inhalation, placing your hands on your hips and lift your torso upward with a straight spine, again hinging at the hips.

Hinge from the hip joint, not the waist.

Flexibility and Your Breath

Your breath plays a big role in the flexibility and depth of your stretches. Go back to the standing forward bend to find out. Bend at the waist and try to touch the mat as you hold your breath. Now do the same as you inhale. Holding your breath tightens and restricts your muscles, reducing your stretch.

Once you've gotten into the habit of breathing deeply, fully and slowly, begin to breathe into your muscles. This isn't as complicated as it may sound to those of you who've never tried it. Simply imagine your breath moving the muscle you're stretching. If you're having problems with this, start by breathing into the muscles of the chest and upper back; this will be easiest, since these muscles directly surround your lungs.

As you focus your attention on the muscle you're stretching while breathing deeply and fully, you'll begin to feel the muscle relax more and more with each exhale. You'll be able to gain more flexibility in that muscle more quickly than you would if you simply stretched it without paying attention to your breath and relaxing.

Yoga Poses for Flexibility

All yoga poses focus on flexibility to some extent. Here are two that can help enhance flexibility and range of motion where you need it most for your golf game.

Yoga Pose 16: Intense Side Stretch

A flexibility-oriented pose that can help your swing, the Intense Side Stretch safely stretches your spine, shoulders, hips, and hamstrings, strengthens the legs, improves posture and sense of balance, stimulates the abdominal organs and aids digestion.

How to do it:

1. Stand with your feet 3½ to 4 feet apart. Rest your hands on your hips. Turn your right foot inward 45 to 60 degrees and your left foot outward 90

degrees. Turn your body and hips toward the left foot. Align the left heel with the instep of the right foot. Firm your thighs and turn your left thigh outward, so the center of the left kneecap is in line with the center of the left ankle.

2. Exhale and square your pelvis as much as possible to the front edge of your mat. As the right hip turns forward, the left hip presses back. Firm your shoulder blades against your back, lengthen your tailbone toward the floor, and arch your upper torso back slightly. Stretch your head away from your tailbone.

3. With another exhalation, lean forward from the hips over the left leg. Stop when the torso is parallel to the floor. Press your fingertips to the floor on either side of the left foot. If it isn't possible for you to touch the floor, support your hands on a pair of blocks or the seat of a folding chair. Press the thighs back and lengthen the torso forward, lifting through the top of the sternum.

4. Hold your torso and head parallel to the floor for a few breaths. Then, if you have the flexibility, bring the front torso closer to the top of the thigh, but don't round forward from the waist to do this. Eventually the front torso will rest down on the thigh. Hold your maximum position for 15 to 30 seconds, then with an inhalation, come up by pressing actively through the back heel and pointing the tailbone down. Then go to the other side by rotating the feet in the other direction and repeating the steps.

For another golf-friendly flexibility pose, meet Seated Spinal Twist, which stretches your shoulders, spine, upper and lower back, hips and abdomen.

Yoga Pose 17: Seated Spinal Twist

If this pose seems a little tricky to get everything in position, you're not the first yogi to ever feel that way. Just be sure you are twisting away from the foot on the side you are turning toward; for example, if you are twisting to the left, you'll be turning away from your left foot.

How to do it:

1. From a seated position with both legs outstretched, bend your right knee, cross the leg over the left leg, and bring the sole of your right foot to the floor on the outside of the left thigh.

2. Bend the left knee, and place the side of the left foot near the right buttock. Beginners: If you cannot bend your leg into the ideal position to get your foot back by your hip, you may also keep your leg extended as shown above.

3. Inhale and stretch up from the crown of your head, so that the spine lengthens. Lift the left arm up and over the right knee, placing the back of the upper left arm (tricep) on the outside of the right knee.

4. Exhale and twist the to the right, with the left elbow to the outside of the right knee and the right palm to the floor, just behind your tailbone.

5. Look out over the right shoulder if you want, but

don't overturn the neck – the twist originates in the belly region, not the neck.

6. On each inhale, draw the spine taller, and on each exhale, twist a little farther.

7. Try to keep the sole of your right foot flat on the floor.

8. When you release the pose, take a slight counter-twist to the opposite direction.

9. Release the legs and switch their position as you prepare to twist to the other side.

Yoga Pose 18: Cow Face

Hip stretch prep for Cow Face pose

How to do it:

1. Sit on the floor with your legs out in front of you. Bend your left leg and bring the left heel to the outside of the right hip. Bring the right leg up and

over the left leg, and put the right heel as close as possible to the left hip joint, stacking the knees over each other or as close to stacking them as you can. Sit evenly on the sit bones. You will definitely feel this in your hip joints. (Figure 2)

2. Inhale and stretch your right arm straight forward, parallel to the floor, palm up. With another inhalation, stretch the arm straight up toward the ceiling, palm turned back. (Figure 2)

Figure 2   *Figure 3*

3. Lift actively through your right arm. Then, with an exhalation, bend the elbow and reach down your back as far as you can, palm toward the spine.

Beginners: hold a towel in the hand of your upper arm, and drape it down your back, giving the hand of the lower arm a prop to grab hold of to help keep the arms in position.

4. Inhale and stretch your left arm straight out to the left, parallel to the floor. Rotate your arm inward; the thumb will turn toward the floor. Then sweep the forearm behind your torso and tuck it behind your lower back, with the left elbow against the left side of your torso. Roll the shoulder back and down, then work the forearm up your back until it is parallel to your spine. The back of your hand will be between your shoulder blades. If possible, hook the right and left fingers, if not, grab the towel that you draped behind your back in step 3 and hold.

5. While holding your fingers or the towel, lift the right elbow toward the ceiling and drop the left elbow toward the floor. Firm your shoulder blades against your back ribs and lift your chest. Try to keep the right arm right beside the right side of your head. Don't forget to breathe.

6. Stay in this pose about 1 minute. Release the arms, uncross the legs, and repeat with the arms and legs

reversed for the same length of time. Remember that whichever leg is on top, the same-side arm is under.

Arm stretch variation with club

How to do it:

1. Stand with your feet hips-width distance apart, knees with a micro bend in them, not locked out.

2. Grab your iron with your right hand, and hold it with your palm facing up.

3. Lift the iron straight up with your palm facing behind you, and bending at the elbow, position the club behind your back with the shank parallel to your spine. Keep your right elbow close to your head.

4. With your left arm, reach back and grab the club, palm facing outward. Keep your left elbow close to your body. Standing up straight, begin to creep your hands together if possible.

5. With hands remaining in position, and straight back, hinge slightly at the hips to emulate your setup stance.

6. Remain here for about 30 seconds, and then switch sides.

See next page for illustration.

Chapter 7: Don't Forget to Breathe!

Yoga's Focus on the Breath Can Improve Your Focus on Your Game

"When the breath wanders the mind also is unsteady. But when the breath is calmed the mind too will be still." – Hatha Yoga Pradipika

Your breath does the all-important task of keeping you alive, and it normally happens without much thought on your part. Unaware, sometimes you breathe deep and full, and sometimes you actually hold your breath. Without understanding the neuromuscular interface, your golf game may be equally erratic as a result of anxiety and stress.

Here's where yoga's attention to fine-tuning your breathing can help; when yoga becomes part of your golf life, every puzzle piece begins to fall into place. Learning to breathe through obstacles keeps the mind calm, creating patience and self-acceptance. Starting with your first breath in yoga, you begin to unravel and eliminate barriers to your success in golf.

Breathing forms the connection between mind and body, and yoga helps you reduce both interior and exterior distractions. Learning to control your breathing will help you better control your game — and your life. When your body is most efficiently using the full power of the breath, amazing things can happen. You'll enjoy increased energy levels, enhanced immunity and a calm, relaxed body and mind.

Yes, it's possible. A concept as seemingly simple as learning to harmonize with your breath can heal, soothe and empower your consciousness. On the course, yoga breathing will help you at tee-off before making a shot, while warming up, and certainly in the rough. Off the course, you can use yoga breathing to lower your general stress level, help fall asleep, maintain your composure as well — you'll be calmer when dealing with intense situations at work, with family and friends, or in an emergency situation or accident.

Welcome to Pranayama

Pranayama is yoga's fancy term for breathing exercises. The word combines the word prana, which means breath or life force energy, and yama, which means to extend, draw out or regulate. Put the two together and you get a term that translates to "breath regulating."

Although the physical poses may be the most well-known element of hatha yoga, yoga masters will tell you they're not the entire point of yoga practice. According to yoga philosophy, the postures exist to open the body for more energy to flow through it and aid in introducing us to deeper states of meditation that lead toward enlightenment, where our minds can grow perfectly still and our lives become content. But just how do we make the leap from Downward Dog to Divine Bliss? Ancient texts give us a clear answer: breathe like a yogi. It has been said that yoga practice is more correctly "breathing with postures," rather than postures with breathing.

So it really is all about the breath. If you don't think you need help in this area, spot check your normal breathing pattern at various points throughout the day. Notice how you breathe while you're driving, sitting at your desk, walking down the block, or playing a round of golf. Unless you've been practicing pranayama, chances are you have one or more unconscious, negative breathing habits.

The Most Common Bad Breathing Habits and How to Correct Them

Improper breathing habits can leave you with low levels of energy, high levels of irritability, a weak immune system and loads of stress.

- Shallow breathing and upper-chest breathing are two of the more common bad breathing habits. Neither allows you to use the full power or capacity of your breath. If your inhalations and exhalations do not move your lower ribs one iota, you're practicing the former. If only your chest moves when you breathe, leaving your abdomen immobile, you're guilty of the latter.

- The worst of the bad breathing habits is breath holding, which consists of either not breathing at all or holding an inhalation for an extended period of time – both of which tending to happen when we are fearful or stressed. When this occurs, you cut yourself off from the most life-sustaining substance known to humanity: oxygen. On the links, short, choppy breathing results in a frustrating, choppy golf game. Master golfers who know how to control the breath know how much it can add to performance.

- Over-breathing (hyperventilation) is breathing too much, which upsets the balance of gases in your system, and happens when you take in too much oxygen and do not expel enough carbon dioxide. Exhalations should take a slightly longer length of time than the inhalations and be completely relaxed, in order to provoke the relaxation response.

- The bad habit of mouth breathing occurs when you totally ignore your nasal passage and only inhale or exhale from your mouth.

- Reverse breathing, as the name implies, actually

reverses the natural movement of your diaphragm and abdomen. An exhalation should leave your abdomen slightly flattened, while an inhalation should slightly raise it. Reverse breathing does the opposite. Watch a baby breathe. Its little shoulders don't go up and down; its little tummy goes in and out.

In building a foundation to establish the basics of breathing, first you come to understand that they are not so much breathing "techniques" as they are methods of establishing basic "breath awareness", and elimination of bad habits and irregularities. Breath awareness is so important that, in a sense, you can say that the whole science of yoga breathing begins and ends with awareness.

Bad breathing habits like to crop up during times of stress, like when you're on the putting green. These include holding the breath; jerky, ragged breathing; short and choppy exhalations; and tensing the muscles in the upper chest, shoulders, and throat, constricting the breath and leaving you gasping for air. Get rid of the stress by learning to literally breathe easy. Think of your breathing rhythm as a lullaby that gently lulls your mind into a state of calm.

Progressive Relaxation Breathing Technique

Here's a simple way to calm your body and keep it quiet during times of stress:

- Go through a step-by-step conscious relaxation

process, starting with intentionally relaxing your jaw, followed by your throat, neck, shoulders, belly, spine, hips and legs.

- Inhale deeply, and imagine the breath reaching to the deepest part of your torso, all the way down to where your lungs actually end, slightly above your waist.

- Exhale deeply and relax.

- Repeat 10 times, scanning your interior landscape for any area in which you might be holding on to tension, and breathe toward that spot.

Breath awareness builds the bridge between the body and the mind. When trying to still the mind it is extremely common to notice muscular tension and exceptionally noisy thoughts. The busy thoughts are actually there all the time, but it is not until you focus and attempt to quiet your mind that you notice how much they are really clamoring.

For better or worse, your nervous system is what is running the show. One of the best ways to regulate your nervous system, and in turn the body and mind, is through the breath. This has been known by yogis for thousands of years, and has also come to be widely known in recent years by the modern medical and psychological community, and now by you, the modern golfer.

A Steady Mind for a Steady Game

Efficient breathing is a must for achieving the cool, calm and collected mindset so integral to an equally cool and calm golf game. An ideal way to practice both efficient breathing habits and calming the mind is with a pranayama exercise where you breathe in, out, and hold the breath for specific counts.

Counting Pranayama Exercise

Close your eyes and breathe using the following count:

- Inhale deeply for four counts;
- hold the breath for four counts;
- exhale fully for six counts;
- pause without breathing for two counts.

Note: If you have high blood pressure or any kind of heart problem, do not hold your breath; just make the inhale and exhale eight counts each.

Allow each muscle in your body to relax, consciously focus on letting go, unwinding and releasing any tension. Use the progressive muscle breathing technique we described above to bring down your tension level a few notches.

Practice this for 5-10 minutes, and notice what a difference it makes. If you find that you get agitated during your counting pranayama breathing exercise, it could possibly be because you are breathing too fast, or forcing the exhale out too hard. If this happens, just make the breathing more gentle.

Chapter 8: Focus and Concentration

"A leading difficulty with the average player is that he totally misunderstands what is meant by concentration. He may think he is concentrating hard when he is merely worrying." – Bobby Jones

Yoga Can Help You Fully Connect

Now that your body is getting stronger and better from developing your swing muscles, core, symmetry, balance, flexibility and breathing, it's time to work on your mind. After all, one of the adages you may have already heard kicking around the course, "Golf is played in the body but won in the mind," calls attention to the focus, concentration and connection you need for a successful game.

It doesn't matter how powerful your swing, how substantial your core or how symmetrical, balanced, flexible and fortified with oxygen your body may be – if your mind is off in la-la land, your game is likely to suffer. Yoga primes your mind for a successful game by helping you develop focus, concentration, and an awareness of and connection to the world around you.

Focus and Concentration

Focus and concentration are two linked concepts, both of which require you to center your full attention on something ... like that ball in front of you.

You've probably played dozens of games where your mind was truly not on the ball but instead galloping off rapidly in dozens of different directions. Perhaps you were pondering what the others in your foursome think of you, what you'll be having for dinner, sex, what you just had for breakfast, yesterday's fight with your spouse, or tomorrow's big work presentation. Whatever the thoughts were, they did not include that little golf ball you were trying to get to an equally small and specific location, the cup.

Even if your wildly rambling mind does not totally destroy your game, it can at least annihilate the pleasure you could experience from being present in the "here and now." Here is a simple exercise that can help corral rambling thoughts by fine-tuning your ability to focus and concentrate.

Exercise for Focus and Concentration

Grab a golf ball, any golf ball, and sit comfortably in a quiet location where you won't be disturbed for at least 5 to 10 minutes. Shut off your cell phone, close the door, and do your best to otherwise eliminate any potential distractions or interruptions.

• Start doing the Counting Pranayama exercise you

just learned. If you missed it, here it is again: Close your eyes and breathe deeply, then: Inhale deeply for four counts, hold for four counts, exhale fully for six counts, hold for two counts. (If you have high blood pressure or any kind of heart problem, do not hold your breath, just make the inhale and exhale eight counts each.) Allow each muscle in your body to relax, consciously focus on letting go, unwind and release any tension. Scan through your body with your inner awareness, and soften any holding or tightness to bring down your tension level several notches.

- Open your eyes and place your awareness on the golf ball in your hand. Gaze at it. Examine it. Examine it deeply, noticing the color, texture, weight and any specific details. Note the color and size of the writing, the depth and the pattern of the dimples, any mars, scuffs or other traits. Continue to examine the ball deeply for a few minutes. If you are aware of any self-induced judging or comparing, just breathe and bring your awareness back to the ball. If your mind starts to wander notice it when it does and, without criticizing yourself, gently bring your concentration back to the ball. (This is not easy, but who said being in "the zone" would be?)

- Now close your eyes and imagine the ball as you just examined it. Try to recall every aspect you noted with your eyes open. After several moments of golf ball recall, open your eyes.

Congrats! You've just completed your first focus and concentration exercise, two concepts that you can now put into play in your next game. Focus on the pin, focus on the ball, and concentrate on where you want the ball to go. Feel the ground under your feet. Breathe ... and take your shot.

Dangers of the Rambling Mind

A rambling mind can not only damage your game with distracting thoughts about dinner and strategizing a raise, but it can kill it with conscious, analytical intrusions. This logical, scientific, left-brained mind can barge its way in when you're truly feeling in "the zone," or enjoying the focus and concentration that comes from being in the moment and paying acute attention to your game. When it does, the analytical mind, begging for attention, begins by telling you your swing might work a little better if you stand like this, or your putt be a little more accurate if you hit like that, or otherwise offering unwanted tips on things your body is already doing naturally, thanks to the tons of practice you've already put into your golf game.

Quash it. Tell it to take a flying leap into the nearby lake and go back to your concentration on the ball, the game, the task in front of you. Deep breathing and recalling the golf ball concentration exercise can both help with shutting off the analytical mind and letting your awareness, focus, and concentration return to the ball, and the joy of the game.

Another way to keep your mind on track is to create a little ritual to perform before each game or even before each hole. Gentle stretching, deep breathing, and counting backwards from 20 with your eyes closed are all great ways to prime your mind to stay focused on your game.

Yoga Pose for Focus and Concentration

To be effective, every yoga poses requires focus and concentration, especially the balance poses. Tree Pose, which you met in Chapter 5, is an ideal example, as is Eagle Pose. This standing pose balances you on one foot, with the other foot wrapped around the calf of the standing leg, and your arms bent at the elbows and intertwined in front of you.

Not only will this pose help you concentrate (or you will not be able to do it), but the posture loosens and stretches the muscles in the upper back and shoulders. This pose quickly relieves tension that develops from working at your desk all day.

Yoga Pose 18: Eagle

How to do it:

1. Stand with your legs shoulder-width apart.

2. Exhale and extend your arms in front of you, parallel to the floor, as you widen your back. Inhale and cross your arms in front of you with the left arm above the right, and bend your elbows. Ensure your left elbow is nestled in the crook of your right arm as you raise your forearms perpendicular to the floor. Inhale and gently place the backs of your hands together.

3. Exhale and move your left hand to your left and your right hand to your right so the palms face each other. Inhale and press the palms together as closely as you can. Exhale and lift your elbows as you stretch your fingers toward the ceiling.

4. Exhale and bend your knees slightly. Shifting your weight, balance on your left foot, then lift up your right leg, and cross your right thigh over your left thigh. (Figure 1)

5. Point the toes of your right foot toward the floor, bring the foot back, and hook the top of it behind the lower portion of your left calf. (Figure 3)

Inhale and concentrate on your balance. If you find that you cannot wrap your foot behind the calf, just touch your toes to the ground on the outside of the standing leg.

6. Continue to inhale and exhale as you hold the pose for at least 15 seconds. Unwind back to standing with an exhale and repeat on other side.

If you cannot tuck your foot behind the standing leg, keep the toes touching the ground.

Chapter 9: All About Attitude

A Bad Attitude Generally Results in a Bad Game. Yoga Philosophy Can Help You Fix Both

"When we think of failure; failure will be ours. If we remain undecided nothing will ever change. All we need to do is want to achieve something great and then simply to do it. Never think of failure, for what we think will come about." – Maharashi Mahesh

When you wake up each morning you immediately have two choices. You can either open your eyes with wonder, ready to embrace the gifts the day will bring, or you can start worrying about all the annoying tasks clogging up your agenda. Can you guess which attitude will result in a good day, and which one will position you for hours of living hell?

The same choice applies to your golf game:

- If you go onto the course with the aim of embracing and enjoying the experience, regardless of the outcome, you can have the best game of your life, even if it comes with the worst score you've ever seen.

- On the flip side, if you go onto the course scowling about the hazards and challenges in store, you're likely to have one of the worst games of your life, even if you achieve the best score you've ever had.

It Really Is All About Attitude

Yoga teachings put a vast emphasis on attitude, with the goal of cultivating a healthy one that helps you remove the emotional and mental rubble that keeps your true, blissful Self buried. Some teachers say that the Self enjoys every experience, and that it is only our context and judgment that detracts from our enjoyment of any and all experiences.

Once you connect with that non-judgmental Self, you can enjoy the soul-satisfying experiences that Self has in every aspect of your daily life, even if that aspect is a very poor-scoring golf game.

So what do you have to do to experience this sublime unveiling? Why, work on your attitude, of course!

Yoga's "10 Commandments" and How They Relate to Golfers

In addition to improving your golf game, yoga aims to bring enlightenment through what some call its "10 Commandments." While these "rules" will not dictate whether or not you go to heaven or hell, they can make your life a kind of heaven on Earth by helping you cultivate a positive attitude. The list contains five yamas, which focus on restraint; and five niyamas, or observances to heed throughout your life.

Ready? Here come the 10 concepts and what they can mean to you.

1. Non-Harming (Ahimsa)

This yama is all about not harming anyone or anything in thought, deed or action, including your precious Self. (No, this is not sarcasm. To be a master at anything, including golf, you must have high self-esteem and a belief that you are can be great.) This concept is about purging most of the irritability, hostility and violence in your being and replacing it with inner peace. Get rid of the negativity so you can make room for peace.

2. Truthfulness (Satya)

Here's where you stop fudging reality and fooling yourself, stop confusing the truth with your opinion. Life gets easier right away.

3. Non-Stealing (Asteya)

Even though you're (hopefully) not sneaking someone else's putter into your golf bag, you can steal people's time by being late or their happiness by being a real downer.

4. Energy Moderation (Brahmacharya)

Physical indulgences fall into this category, including gorging on foods, too much TV watching, overindulgence in sex, blasting loud music, and going on endless shopping sprees, which are in violation of this important, stabilizing concept. Yes, a 24-hour gambling marathon is another violation of the brahmacharya, otherwise known as "too much partying."

5. Non-Grasping (Aparigraha)

Humans' penchant for "more, more, more" and their consequent greed and neediness is at constant odds with the idea of non-grasping. Stop lusting after and coveting everything you see, and get rid of the things that are no longer useful. If you keep your home and life stuffed with old junk, there's no room for new treasures to come in. Let go...

6. Purity (Saucha)

Purity refers to intention as related to your actions, not a judgmental or religious connotation. Purity is the spirit in which you do things. You cannot always be aware of the consequences of all your actions, but you can be aware of your intentions. If you want your partners to have as good a time on the course as you want to have (even though you hope their scores are higher than yours), that is purity in action.

7. Contentment (Samtosha)

Contentment comes simply from acceptance. Take

a cue from the somewhat overused adage "It is what it is," and you're on the right track. Just because you accept something doesn't mean you have to like it, but if you want any inner serenity you do have to acknowledge that life is the way it is, whether you like it or not. Yes, this even counts for a really bad golf score. The famous Serenity Prayer of Alcoholics Anonymous is a great example of a path to contentment. "God grant me the serenity to accept the things I cannot change; courage to change the things I can; and wisdom to know the difference."

8. Right Effort (Tapas)

Another slightly overused phrase – "doing the next right thing" – helps explain this concept. Being willing, eager and open to doing the work that enhances your life is what tapas is all about. You've already demonstrated this concept with your willingness to do the work it takes to learn more about how yoga can enhance your golf game! Another way to understand this is the concept of consistency: the cheerful willingness to do your warmup drills, practice your yoga, still the antics of your wandering mind and be gentle with yourself for fluffing a shot.

9. Self-Study (Svadhyaya)

Here's where you turn your attention inward to discover your true nature and your true Self. It's also the only real way to find happiness, yoga philosophy says, as happiness never comes from outside sources but always from within. You could also think of this niyama as "remembering to be aware." Snap yourself on the wrist with a rubber band if you forget this one.

10. Dedication to the Highest (Ishvara Pranidhana)

Whether you believe in God, several gods or no God, a Great Creator, or simply a mysterious Higher Energy that created and reigns supreme throughout the universe, aligning yourself with this power is the ultimate step in your enlightenment that can do absolute wonders for your attitude! Ishvara pranidhana provides a pathway through the obstacles of our ego toward our divine nature: grace, peace, unconditional love, clarity and freedom.

Begin Living the Yogic Lifestyle

Now that you're aware of the 10 yamas and niyamas, your next goal is taking them with you everywhere you go, including on the golf course, and watch your life start an upward spiral of calm consistency and serene acceptance. Focusing on the concepts in meditation is a great step, and you've already experienced a form of meditation when you focused on the golf ball in Chapter 8.

Here's how to start integrating these qualities into your life even more effectively:

• Choose one yama or niyama on which you will concentrate.

- Sit quietly in a straight-backed chair, or on the floor with your knees open, your spine straight, and your shoulders rolled back. Close your eyes and take a moment to become aware of your breathing, with deep inhalations in and out through your nose.

- Let your palms rest face up on your knees, as you soften your chest, open your heart, and begin to relax all your muscles. Now concentrate your thoughts on your concept, such as purity of inten- tion, spending as much time as you need to truly grasp what it means to you. Just relax and ponder it. You simply cannot do this meditation wrong, because what it means to you is completely personal.

- Repeat with each concept at different medita- tion sessions throughout the week, starting each morning with a few minutes of meditation to help hone your attitude for the day.

The way to incorporate these concepts into your life fully is to practice them daily, even if only for a few moments. Keep them in mind in all you do, every action you take, every golf ball you hit. Keep them in mind when you are tempted to be catty to your golf mate, or jealous of a rival, or angry that your game is going sour. Stop yourself, step back, and figure out which yoga guideline needs your attention. And as always, don't forget to breathe!

Chapter 10: Overcoming Obstacles

Yoga Transforms Sand Traps and Other Hazards into Welcome Challenges

"We find our energies are actually cramped when we are overanxious to succeed." – Michel de Montaigne

When your golf ball smacks into a sand trap or plops smartly into a lake, your first reaction is probably not a very pleasant one. You may immediately feel a surge of disappointment, shame or even rage. You may suddenly erupt in a string of profanities, start kicking at the turf, or even begin to belittle yourself with phrases like, "How could I be so stupid?!"

This type of reaction only serves to make the situation worse. It clouds your thinking and actions with negativity and totally destroys the balance, harmony, flexibility and positive attitude you have used yoga to enhance. On top of all that, it makes you look pretty foolish.

Yoga's Nine Hindrances to Loving Your Life

Yoga is about overcoming obstacles, from physical

things like sand traps and lakes, to the deeper, spiritual variety that hinders your growth, development and overall happiness. For hundreds of years, we as humans have endeavored to improve our relations to ourselves, God and each other. Times may be different, and the world may change, but generation after generation, we come across the same pitfalls of humanity.

In fact, yoga philosophy has a ready-made slate of nine obstacles, known as Antaraya, which everyone faces throughout their lives. Here they are:

1. Illness (Vyadi)

Mental, physical and spiritual maladies all count as vyadi, as do sicknesses that stem from chronic negativity.

2. Languor, Mental Stagnation (Styana)

Hate your desk job so much you only sit around doing the least amount of work possible to not get fired? You may be having a bout of styana.

3. Doubt (Samshaya)

Afraid to quit your job and try something new because you're sure you're just not good enough? Samshaya has you by the throat.

4. Sloth, Fatigue (Alasya)

Maybe you're not too full of doubt to quit your job, but too lazy to even start a job hunt for something new.

5. Dissipation, Overindulging (Avirati)

Don't worry, you can always drink, eat, or shop your woes away, bingeing on junk food and shoes to make yourself feel better. Right?

6. Heedlessness, Lack of Foresight (Pramada)

Thoughtless or unkind remarks, casually tossed off, fall into this category, as well as Foot-in-the-Mouth Syndrome. Also, if you would have thought about your shot for a moment, you may have seen you were angled smack dab toward the sand trap.

7. False Views, Illusions (Bhrantidarshana)

No matter how many times you say it, your golf game may not really be on par with Arnold Palmer's.

8. Lack of Perseverance (Alabdhabhumikatva)

If you're not as good as Palmer, you may as well just give up!

9. Instability, Regression (Anavasthitatva)

Your string of obscenities and throwing a golf club are fine examples of anavasthitatva.

The Nine Hindrances (Antaraya) are not optional. Like it or not, they are inevitable concepts that will crop up again and again throughout your life. The better you are at overcoming them, the less frequently you may see them. And yoga can help make you a conquering hero.

Some Thoughts on Negative Thoughts

Negative thoughts can make overcoming obstacles next to impossible; they can ruin your day or an entire life. While you may not be able to snap your fingers and make them disappear, you can get rid of them using various techniques.

- One is to acknowledge them, thank them for being there, and then send them on their way. "While I've enjoyed your company," you can tell them, "it's time for you to leave, since you're taking up way too much space in my head."
- Replacing negative thoughts with positive ones is another helpful tactic. The next time your ball blasts into a sand trap, think of at least one or two positive aspects about the situation. Perhaps the sand reminds you of blissfully being at the beach, or the view of the golf course from the sand trap is simply breathtaking.

Mindfulness

Another concept ingrained in yoga is that of mindfulness. As mentioned earlier in the discussion on the niyama of self-study, mindfulness is an awareness of everything around you, acceptance of things exactly as they are, and opening to where you fit into the overall picture.

Mindfulness focuses on sensory perceptions rather than internal thoughts and allows you to observe how you can interact with the world in the absence of making any judgments. You can cultivate it by paying attention, feeling the feelings in your body, focusing on balance to steady your heart and your head. By eliminating judgment, you can freely offer compassion to all the living things around you – as well as yourself.

Putting it All Together

The next time you hit a ball into a sand trap, take a long, deep breath. Tell the negative thoughts that pop into your head that they are taking up way too much room, and find a few positive thoughts to take their place. Then shift your focus away from your emotions and onto your sensory perceptions. Step away from the emotional turmoil and simply observe the way your mind works and how your body feels. Pay attention, balance your heart and mind, offer yourself compassion.

Then get over to that sand trap and chip your ball out of there!

Yoga Pose for Overcoming Obstacles

Yoga Pose 19: Camel

All poses can benefit from mindfulness and paying attention to the small adjustments you need to make to sustain the pose for an extended period. Backbends are king for helping you overcome obstacles, and Camel or modified Camel is a great one with which to start. If you have any issues with your lower back, go slowly and gently. In addition, beginner or advanced, the yogi should think of lifting his or her chest, and avoiding compressing the back of the waist.

How to do it:

1. Kneel on the floor with your knees hip-width apart and thighs perpendicular to the floor. Firm up but don't harden your buttocks. Press your shins and the tops of your feet firmly into floor.

2. Place the base of your palms on your sacrum at the tops of the buttocks with your fingers pointed down. Lengthen your spine by lifting the torso upward from the crown of the head.

3. Inhale and lift your heart gently toward the sky, squeezing your shoulder blades and elbows behind you, and look up. Gently begin to lean back as far as you are comfortable. In the beginning, keep

your head upright and look forward, as you get more advanced with this pose, you will begin to bend your head back also.

4. As you lean back a little farther, place one hand at a time on the heels, while keeping the thighs perpendicular to the floor. Twist slightly to one side to reach the hand back, and once one hand is on the heel, bring the other hand to the other heel. If you are not able to lean back far enough to reach your heels without compressing your lower back, turn your toes under and elevate your heels.

5. Make sure that your lower front ribs aren't protruding sharply toward the ceiling, which tightens the belly and compresses the lower back. Lift the lower back ribs away from the pelvis to keep the lower spine as long as possible. Press your palms firmly against your heels, with the bases of the palms on the heels and the fingers pointing toward the toes. You can keep your neck in a relatively neutral position, neither flexed nor extended, or drop your head back. But be careful not to strain your neck and harden your throat.

6. Stay in this pose anywhere from 30 seconds to 1 minute. To exit, bring your hands back to the back of the pelvis. Inhale and lift the head and torso up. If your head is back, lead with your heart to come up. Rest in Child's Pose for a few breaths.

Left—Beginner: Look up with hands on hips
Right—Intermediate: Lift chest and lean back slightly

Advanced: Lean back far enought to place hands on heels.

Yoga Pose 20: Corpse Pose

The final pose that does more than refresh!

The ideal way to finish your practice is in a relaxed yoga pose, the aptly named Corpse pose. You can't get much more relaxed than this, in which you simply lie back and practice letting go. (Hint: it can be harder than it seems, because a corpse doesn't think about the drive to the office or home, what's for dinner, or how it might have missed something on the latest P&L report.)

This pose is done at the end of every yoga session to allow the body to rest completely and regenerate, reaping the benefits from all the stretching, breathing, strengthening and balancing that preceded it. You should always try to finish your yoga session with the Corpse Pose, even if you only have time for a few minutes of it.

Because it's so relaxing, some people never get beyond Step 5 below, because they fall asleep. But let's give it a shot.

How to do it:

1. Start seated on the mat with your legs bent and feet flat on the floor. Inhale deeply then exhale, leaning back onto your forearms and slightly

lifting your pelvis off the mat. Place the sacrum flat on the mat by tucking the tailbone toward the foot of the mat. Deeply inhale and slowly extend one leg, then the other, as you soften the groins and turn the feet slightly outward. Exhale deeply as you soften your lower back and feel your body sink gently onto the mat.

2. Inhale and use your hands to lift the base of your skull away from your neck as you soften the muscles in the back of the neck, releasing them toward the tailbone. Exhale deeply as you broaden the base of your skull and ensure your body is symmetrical on the mat.

3. Deeply inhale and reach both arms toward the ceiling as you rock your body slightly side to side to broaden your back against the mat. Deeply exhale and release your arms to the mat, turning the thumbs slightly outward and resting the backs of the hands on the mat.

4. Deeply inhale and then exhale, softening your tongue, your facial muscles, your scalp and the skin on your forehead. Close your eyes and let them sink back into your skull; allow your brain to settle and do the same.

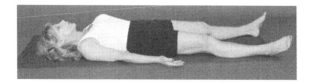

5. For the first couple of minutes focus on your breathing. Breathe deeply and slowly, being mindful of each inhalation and exhalation. Deeply inhale, then completely relax and let the exhale flow out. Extend your exhalations by a second or two, making them longer than your inhalations. Pause slightly after each deep exhalation, languishing in this moment of stillness and quiet. Inhale deeply and breathe with your whole body, feeling the breath move the belly and slightly rock the hips, shoulders and spine. Feel the breath filter through every muscle and organ in your body, calming and soothing every cell. Exhale deeply, once again feeling it in every cell.

6. Now just begin to let go. Do not focus on the breath; allow it to become soft and natural, and simply observe where it goes. Let yourself relax completely. If you have time constraints, you may want to set an alarm in case you drift off.

7. After 5-15 minutes of practicing Corpse Pose, slowly start to bring your awareness back into the room, and into your body. Wiggle your fingers and toes a bit. When ready, come out of the pose with a deep inhalation as you gently roll to one side and bring yourself to seated position on the mat.

After Corpse pose, the traditional ending to a yoga session might include sitting in an upright position with the palms together in front of the heart, focusing your awareness on gratitude for the gift of serenity, strength and composure your practice has produced, and letting go of the effort that it took to produce it.

The salutation "Namaste" is often exchanged, which means, "The light within me greets (or acknowledges) the light within you." If you are not practicing with a teacher, acknowledge the light within yourself.

Conclusion

"When I swing at a golf ball right, my mind is blank and my body is loose as a goose." – Sam Snead

"Be at least as interested in what goes on inside you as what happens outside. If you get the inside right, the outside will fall into place." – Eckhart Tolle

Now that you've learned the inter-connectedness of your muscles, bones, flexibility, mind, energy, breath, awareness and attitude, soon it will be time to get on the links and start letting go of everything that you've been learning, and simply PLAY in the most literal sense of the word.

Like the Zen monks who practice the art of archery only to hone their physical and mental abilities, you will toss away all the techniques you've been applying, and simply let your body do what the hours of practice has taught it to do — play brilliant golf.

The players you most admire might have a few advantages over you. They might be younger, fitter, or have more fast-twitch muscles, but they are human just like you. The reason they play so well is that they have mastered several aspects of the game, and many of them excel at most aspects. That does not mean that you cannot improve in many of the areas that may have eluded you up until now.

Golf and yoga give you the opportunity to improve your entire life when you use them as a mirror. As Hale Irwin puts it, "Golf is the loneliest sport. You're completely alone with every conceivable opportunity to defeat yourself. Golf brings out your assets and liabilities as a person. The longer you play, the more certain you are that a man's performance is the outward manifestation of who, in his heart, he really thinks he is." It is the very same with yoga.

Good luck on the links!

Yoga Definition

Yoga has become so mainstream in America, almost everyone has heard of it and its benefits, but if asked to explain what it is, cannot do so. I've included a simple explanation here of what yoga is and what it can do for you.

Yoga is a systematic practice of physical exercise, breath control, relaxation, diet, positive thinking and meditation aimed at developing harmony in the body, mind, spirit and environment. The practice entails low-impact physical activity, postures (asanas), breathing techniques (pranayama), relaxation and meditation. Most people are familiar with the physical poses or yoga positions but don't know that yoga involves much more self-development practices to evolve as a whole person.

In the health fields, yoga techniques are being applied in health programs, substance abuse treatment programs, and as complementary treatment for diseases such as anxiety disorders, depression, coronary heart disease, cancer, and HIV/AIDS. Yoga has emerged as a comprehensive, easy, low-cost self-help approach to well-being.

The origin is a Sanskrit word Yog meaning union. Yoga is a union of the organ systems in the body with the consciousness in the mind. Philosophically, yoga produces a union of body, mind, and energy to bring about a state of equanimity or calmness.

Progressing to an even more advanced state, blending science and philosophy, one experiences a union of body, mind, internal energy, and the all-pervading cosmic energy, resulting in better physical health, mental control and, ultimately, self-realization, or the awareness and implications of one's true Divine nature.

Glossary of Yoga Terms

- Asana: a low physical impact posture practiced in yoga to stretch or engage muscles, and affect glands and organs
- Ashtanga: style of hatha yoga practice that emphasizes strength and is characterized by one pose being connected to another, and uses the breath extensively; also known as power yoga
- Aum (or Ohm): Sanskrit word meaning "all" represents the omnipresence of Paramatma (the supreme spirit)
- Chakra: a point of intersection of the main channels of energy flow in the body (Chakras regulate the functioning of the body and correspond to the major endocrine glands in the body.)
- Guru: teacher; spiritual preceptor
- Hatha yoga: the path of yoga that starts with the practice of physical postures (asanas)
- Karma yoga: the path of yoga that starts with emphasis on performing one's duty (action)
- Kundalini: latent energy lying dormant at the base of the spinal column
- Kundalini yoga: the path of yoga that starts with meditation
- Maharishi: a great sage
- Mudra: a seal; a sealing posture

- Nadi: a tubular organ of the subtle body through which the energy flows
- Nauli: a process in which the abdominal muscles and organs are made to move in a surging motion
- Patanjali: name of the first writer of yoga philosophy
- Prana: breath; life; vitality
- Pranayama: the rhythmic regulation of breath
- Raja yoga: the path of yoga that starts with psychic control of the mind
- Rishi: an inspired sage
- Sadhana: quest
- Surya: the sun
- Yoga: Yoga literally means union; the aim of yoga is to practice the means by which the human soul may be completely united with the supreme spirit
- Yogi: (male or female, such as the way "actor" is used) one who follows the path of yoga

Acknowledgments

There are a number of people to whom I am indebted who helped in the creation of this book. First, I want to thank my husband Michael Garver for encouraging me in all my endeavors, and for taking the wonderful photos that illustrate the postures.

Heartfelt thanks to:

My researcher and collaborator, Ryn Gargulinski, as well as my editors and proofreaders, Sue Loiseau and Susan Salter.

The friends and colleagues who helped me come up with a title and offered suggestions for content, Amy Lacombe, Bonnie and Steve Walker, Lynda Montano, Victoria Sackstaeder, Jimmy Jordan, Jim and Frances Fitzpatrick, Craig and Jane Angell, Roy Teel, Jr., Stefan Pollack, William Ostedt, and Mark Havenner

My "muse," Stephen Mitchell, who kept needling me to make it better until it was right.

My excellent and patient yoga models, Bruno Lacombe and Don Dawson.

My colleague Laren Bright, who supports me in all my projects, harebrained and otherwise.

And lastly, my colleague Ellen Reid, who taught me what makes a book "excellent."

About the Author

An internationally recognized authority in the field of personal growth, Patricia Bacall teaches people how to live happier, more fulfilling and creative lives. Her classes and seminars attract people of all backgrounds and ages from all parts of the world.

As a personal coach and seminar leader, Patricia is known for her ability to empower clients to live the lives they want – not the lives they seem to have "fallen into." And her participants respond, often commenting on the clarity of Patricia's communication and her thorough knowledge of her subject matter.

With her engaging, positive approach, Patricia assists the healing process by teaching people to see themselves as strong and unique individuals, and to use that empowerment as the means to achieve their dreams and goals.

A journey of discovery

Patricia's journey of educating individuals to improve their health and well-being began in 1980. As a personal trainer, she realized the importance of the mind-body connection and the healing benefits of yoga. So Patricia became a certified yoga instructor and massage therapist.

During the late '80s, Patricia added to her expertise by mastering the Vivation breathwork technique, which uses a simple, yet powerful, breathing process to help people create resolution of their most negative emotions. Working with Jim Leonard, the founder of Vivation®, she became one of the best-trained Vivation breathwork professionals in the United States. Patricia uses the Vivation technique in her workshops and private practice to "supercharge" the healing process by uncovering and resolving suppressed emotions.

To round out her education in body, mind and spirit wellness, Patricia studied yoga, Pilates, massage and Emotional Freedom Techniques (EFT), and holds several credentials in these disciplines. She serves on the board of the Associated Vivation Professionals in the United States and is a contributor to health publications and websites on the subjects of emotional overeating, physical vitality, overcoming negativity, energy work and yoga.

Explore Patricia's wellness collection

Additional books and CDs on health and well-being by Patricia Bacall are available at Amazon and other online retailers.

- <u>Easy Weight Loss Yoga: 12 Best Poses to Get Lean, Strong and Calm.</u> Learn how yoga helps the glands, organs, and systems in your body increase metabolism and encourage burning fat for energy.
- <u>Loving Yourself Thin:</u> Address the underlying emotions that cause you to overeat, eat for reasons

other than hunger and keep unwanted weight on.

- The New Weight Loss Blueprint: Discover which foods support healthy functioning of your entire system, so that weight loss occurs naturally and effortlessly.

- Vivation Breathwork 2-CD audio set: Supercharge your life with this technique for extreme emotional healing.

- Loving Yourself Thin with Vivation Breathwork 2-CD audio set: Heal negative emotions to achieve your ideal body without dieting or deprivation. Theory and guided, coached one-hour session.

For more information, visit: www.vivationusa.com

Thank you for reading this book. I hope you enjoyed it and if you did, I'd be exceedingly grateful if you would leave a positive review.

If you did not, please direct your comments to info@benesserra.com before you leave a negative review. In addition, if you have any comments, (corrections, clarifications) that you feel would improve this book, please write.

Thank you!

Patricia Bacall

June, 2013